D0857554

A CAREER AS AN

AIRCRAFT MECHANIC AND SERVICE TECHNICIAN

Jobs for
REBUILDING AMERICA™

A CAREER AS AN
AIRCRAFT
MECHANIC
AND
SERVICE
TECHNICIAN

Rosen
YA

TAMRA B. ORR

New York

Published in 2019 by The Rosen Publishing Group, Inc.
29 East 21st Street, New York, NY 10010

Library of Congress Cataloging-in-Publication Data

Names: Orr, Tamra, author.
Title: A career as an aircraft mechanic and service technician / Tamra B. Orr.
Description: New York : Rosen Publishing, 2019 | Series: Jobs for rebuilding America | Includes bibliographical references and index. | Audience: Grades 7–12.
Identifiers: LCCN 2017052948| ISBN 9781508179948 (library bound) | ISBN 9781538381847 (pbk.)
Subjects: LCSH: Airplanes—Maintenance and repair—Vocational guidance—Juvenile literature. | Aviation mechanics (Persons)—Juvenile literature.
Classification: LCC TL671.9 .O764 2019 | DDC 629.134/6023—dc23
LC record available at https://lccn.loc.gov/2017052948

Manufactured in the United States of America

CONTENTS

INTRODUCTION

You find your seat, stow a carry-on in the overhead compartment, and then sit down. Slowly the seats all around you fill up. You look out the window at the shiny wing below and marvel at how something that looks so big on the ground can fly so elegantly thousands of feet up in the sky.

You buckle your seat belt, as the plane begins to taxi down the runway. The engine roars and you feel the strength vibrating all around you as you are pressed back into the seat. It's both an everyday and extraordinary experience. You rise up off of the ground, defying gravity. Within seconds the trees, cars, and buildings are fading. You are enveloped by clouds.

Flying seems like a modern miracle, not least because it is so

A crew of mechanics work on a plane inside a hangar. Besides those actually piloting the plane, mechanics and technicians are also crucial in making the multibillion-dollar aviation industry safe and reliable.

hard to accept that something so big and heavy manages to lift up off of the ground in the first place. After all, an average airplane weighs hundreds of thousands of pounds. Thousands more come from the passengers, crew, and countless pieces of luggage on board. Even more comes from the gallons of gasoline inside the fuel tanks. Some of the largest planes end up weighing an astonishing million pounds (453,592 kilograms).

And yet these huge metal tubes still manage to fly. Every day, according to the Federal Aviation Administration (FAA), there are five thousand planes in the sky at any given moment. Planes are landing and taking off 24/7 from the country's 19,601 private and public airports. An astounding 2,586,582 passengers fly worldwide every single day.

Being on an airplane that is having a problem can be truly frightening. Fortunately, mechanical problems rarely result in any injuries or deaths—just lots of delays. According to Bob Herbst, former pilot and editor of Airline Financials.com, less than 10 percent of air accidents are caused by mechanical issues. (Just over 5 percent of accidents are caused by bird strikes!) That incredible track record is primarily because of the thousands of skilled, careful aircraft mechanics and service technicians around the world. These men and women are trained to make sure that planes are in good shape every time they take off and after they land. It is their responsibility to repair, replace, and maintain aircraft parts and components. These workers make it possible to fly safely. How do they do it, and what do you need to know in order to do it too? Buckle up your seat belt and find out.

CHAPTER ONE

"GUARDIANS OF AIRWORTHINESS"

Millions of passengers walk onto airplanes every day, find their seats, and sit down more or less confident that the planes they are flying in are safe and well maintained. Every plane, large and small, public and private, is taken care of by a group of dedicated people known as aircraft mechanics and service technicians (AMTs). They are on the front lines of protecting people's lives and ensuring the airlines' bottom lines.

AMTs are the people who check the aircraft from nose to tail. Some brag that they could take apart an engine even if blindfolded. They are the ones who know pneumatic and hydraulic systems backward and forward. They work with the plane's wings and flaps, its landing gear and fuel pumps, and its navigation and communication systems. If they specialize in working each plane's complex electrical systems, AMTs are often referred to as avionics techs.

These amazing skills make AMTs the unsung heroes of our transportation infrastructure. It is little wonder that

The cockpit of an A380 Airbus, the largest passenger jet airliner currently in use, is shown here. Mechanics must be knowledgeable in how a cockpit this complex works in relation to the plane's many systems.

Ronald Donner, chief editor of *Aircraft Maintenance Technology* and executive director of the AMT Society told *Flying*, "We like to think of ourselves as the guardians of airworthiness. Pilots cannot fly an airplane until we, as mechanics, say it's ready to go, and that's a huge responsibility."

TOUCHING THE SKY

Why do some people choose to become aircraft mechanics? For Carlos Alonso, the reason was clear. "Hasn't everyone dreamt of touching the sky with their hands?" he said to *Iberia Plus*. "Even though I know the basic principles of lift, I'm still fascinated by how a structure weighing so much is able to rise above our heads so easily."

Alonso has been in the field for more than twenty years and is grateful for all of the technological improvements that have been made during that time. "We wonder how we managed to do all the inspections and solve all the challenges that we dealt with every day without the means and technology we have today," he stated. "As professionals in the field, we're constantly updating our knowledge and learning new things. We can't forget that behind the safest means of transportation in existence, there's a whole team of professionals that make this 'miracle' possible." Alonso also remembers his first day of work in 1996. "I've got special memories of that day," he recalled. "I was overwhelmed at first, until I finally realized that I was, indeed, part of this incredibly complex team. I'm still astonished."

A PART OF THE NATION'S INFRASTRUCTURE

Although it is easy to think of aircraft only being used to take passengers from one part of the world to the next—and back again—the aviation industry is more than that. Just as it transports people, it also flies products and supplies around the globe. It provides flights to patients in need of critical medical care. It is used by local, state, and federal law enforcement

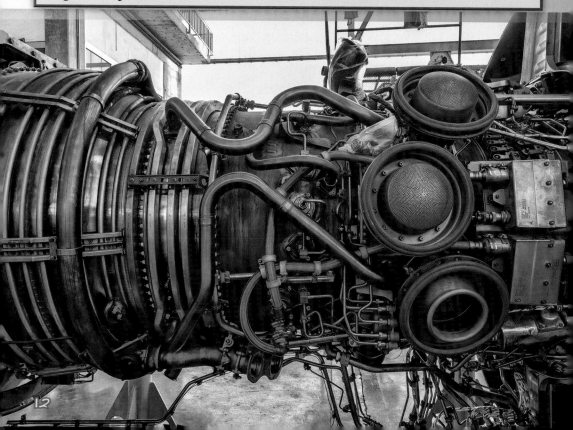

The interior workings of an airplane involve both heavy-duty equipment and sophisticated and delicate engineering. It takes a long time to master servicing engine components.

agencies and helps soldiers complete their military flight training. It provides jobs for almost twelve million people. The aviation industry plays many roles in this country, including:

- Aeromedical flights
- Emergency response/disaster relief/search and rescue
- Law enforcement/border control
- Aerial firefighting support
- Remote population access
- Flight instruction
- Charter services
- Agricultural support
- Aerial surveying
- Oil and mineral exploration
- Pipeline control and inspection
- Express delivery service
- Passenger flights/tourism
- Special aeronautical (skydiving, air shows, etc.)

Commercial aviation, along with all of these other sectors that use aircraft, makes up a huge part of the country's critical infrastructure. The US government defines this type of infrastructure as, "systems and assets, whether physical or virtual, so vital to the United States that the incapacity or destruction of such systems and assets would have a debilitating impact on security, national economic security, national public health or safety, or any combination of those matters." According to the Aerospace Industries Association's report, "Aviation: A Critical Component of National Infrastructure,"

A Boeing 767 cargo plane belonging to the international shipping company DHL takes off at San Diego International Airport. The public relies on mechanics to keep packages on time, as well as their own travels.

the country's "highways of the skies" are definitely a part of these systems. Having them fall into disrepair and lose their ability to function reliably and safely would definitely impact everybody in dire ways.

The United States, like many nations, depends on a system of safe and functioning aircraft. From routine packages, to business travelers getting to their meetings nationwide, to dozens of other functions, the aviation infrastructure keeps the economic wheels turning. Both the newest planes and much older aircraft need to be inspected and repaired as needed. That means having well-trained, knowledgeable, skilled mechanics and service technicians on hand at every airport and airfield.

MEET THE FAA

The Federal Aviation Administration, or FAA, is the agency responsible for the safety of civil aviation. The agency was first created in 1958 as part of the government's Department of Transportation. The FAA is in charge of many aspects of aviation, including monitoring and developing air traffic management, developing programs to control aircraft noise, and making sure that aircraft mechanics and service technicians are trained on the right material in classrooms. The FAA issues mechanics and repairman their certificates. Can you work as an aircraft mechanic without a certificate? The FAA says yes, but, if you don't have one, you can only work when you are supervised by someone who does have one. You are also limited in what you can do, such as inspecting and approving equipment for return to service. "Without a certificate," the FAA states, "you are less likely to advance to the top of the career field."

AIRCRAFT MECHANIC VERSUS AVIONICS TECHNICIAN

Aircraft mechanics and technicians go by several terms. They are also referred to as aircraft technicians or service technicians. There are specific rules of where and when to use these slightly different job titles—aircraft mechanics versus avionics technicians. Here is how their primary responsibilities differ, according to the 2017 *Occupational Outlook Handbook*:

Aircraft Mechanics' Duties	Avionics Technicians' Duties
Diagnose mechanical or electrical problems	Test electronic instruments, using specialized equipment
Repair wings, brakes, electrical systems, and other aircraft components	Interpret flight test data to diagnose malfunctions and performance problems
Replace defective parts using hand or power tools	Assemble electrical components and install software
Examine replacement aircraft parts for defects	Install instrument panels using hand tools, power tools, and soldering irons
Read maintenance manuals to identify repair procedures	Repair or replace malfunctioning components
Test aircraft parts with diagnostic equipment	Keep precise and accurate records of all maintenance and repair work
Inspect completed work to ensure it meets national and FAA performance standards	
Keep precise and accurate records of all maintenance and repair work	

Aircraft technicians work with a variety of systems on an airplane. They inspect components and conduct regular inspections (usually based on FAA regulations). Another of their jobs is determining if aircraft are ready for operation. They also read and apply guidance in maintenance manuals and service bulletins and maintain detailed and thorough documentation of every step they take.

Avionic technicians, on the other hand, tend to focus specifically on planes' electronic systems. For example, they

Besides working hands on to solve immediate mechanical problems, mechanics and technicians must be skilled in reading design and engineering schematics, among other technical materials.

may run tests on a plane's navigation and weather radar to make sure it is working properly. This is a crucial job, since pilots need to trust that their instruments are providing accurate information about where they are going and whether they will run into harsh weather. They fine-tune planes' radio communication systems so that pilots can effectively communicate with others. Avionics technicians generally have to work pretty quickly since the plane needs to be back up in the air as soon as safely possible.

What is at stake is not just the safety of the passengers and crew of a particular plane, though naturally that is priority number one. The trust and confidence that the general public has in aviation also depends on how well thousands of mechanics do their jobs daily.

CHAPTER TWO

GETTING READY FOR THE FUTURE TODAY

*D*o you have the "tinker gene"? Have you have been taking apart every appliance in the house to see what was inside since childhood? You may be the type who tries to figure out how things work and know how to repair them when they don't. Perhaps you

Besides taking the right classes and group activities with like-minded hobbyists, most handy young people will be drawn to tinkering by themselves. It is a good (and fun) way to stay sharp.

daydream about engines and how to improve them. When you look at airplanes flying overhead, in addition to wondering where people are traveling, do you wish you could get a look at the mechanical systems that power such a huge vehicle? If you answered yes to some or all of these questions, a career as an aircraft mechanic or service technician might be just for you. If you suspect this might be the direction you want to go in the near future, you can start preparing right away, in ways both big and small.

INSTANTLY HOOKED

For as long as he could remember, Luke Foreman loved everything to do with flying. He watched airplane shows and documentaries on television and sought out clips online. He was a hands-on learner and enjoyed fixing and building various things, too. When he first heard about a career as an aircraft mechanic, he was "instantly hooked," he told the author. "I knew for certain that this was what I wanted to do."

Foreman attended the Pittsburgh Institute of Aeronautics aviation maintenance school for sixteen months. His classes included physics, math, electronics, and power plant and airframe-related courses. He reminds potential mechanics that organization and attention to detail are extremely important. "In this career field," Foreman explains, "you cannot cut any corners. One simple mistake can cost someone his or her life." He adds that he learned the importance of the paperwork associated with the job. "Paperwork is the hardest part to learn," he admits. "Making sure that everything is in order to meet FAA standards, as well as airline and company standards, is difficult. All maintenance records and aircraft log books are valuable documents. If this paperwork is lost or damaged, the aircraft's value for future resale is cut by at least 50 percent."

In October 2017, Foreman began working for Skywest Airlines, a North American airline headquartered in Utah. He hopes to be working for a major airline such as Delta, American, or United in a lead or supervisor position within ten to fifteen years. His advice for students planning on a career as an aircraft mechanic is simple. "Study all associated books and materials, and study hard to be prepared for the FAA tests," he advises. "In the end, when you are holding your A&P license, there is no better feeling in the world."

AT SCHOOL

The first step is simple: go to school. While attending, take time to talk to your guidance counselor, teachers, and other faculty to see what classes, if any, might cover areas like blueprint reading, computer design and electronics, engine repair, and more. If your school does not offer these classes, ask why. In the past, almost all high schools offered shop class. In this class, students learned the basics of such skills as woodworking, electronics, welding, and, of course, mechanics. They built birdhouses, made lumpy clay cups, and learned how to change the oil in a car.

Over the years, such classes were largely phased out and replaced with college-prep classes. James Stone, director of the National Research Center for Career and Technical Education told *Automotive News*, "It [shop class] became seen as a dumping ground for kids the regular school couldn't figure out what to do with." Fortunately, just in the last decade, that trend has turned around. A growing number of schools are offering shop classes and often have more students signing up than they have room for. If your school has not jumped onto this trend yet, consider meeting with a member of the faculty, guidance counselors, or even the principal and discussing the idea. Do your research first: check out schools that have implemented these classes into their curriculum and ask teachers and students. Even doing so via email could work. Come in with a list of ideas, plans, and steps for what to do next.

Of course, as you explore your options, look beyond your own school. Are there other high schools in the area

Shop classes and other courses where you can really get your hands dirty with tools in a workshop are ideal for building the skills for a mechanical career in aviation.

that offer the classes you want to take? What is involved in enrolling in them or auditing them? Research any vocational or trade high schools in your city or county, and check out their offerings. Edward Bouquillon, superintendent-director of the Minuteman Regional Vocational Technical School told the *Boston Globe*, "At vocational-technical schools, we tell parents we create in the kids a light at the end of the tunnel. We help them discover what they love to do and do well. . .and connect that to a college major or a career."

Former president Barack Obama echoed those thoughts when he spoke at the Worcester Technical High School's 2014 commencement ceremony. He told the graduating students, "Over the past four years, some of you have learned how to take apart an engine and put it back together again. Some of you have learned how to run a restaurant, or build a house, or fix a computer. And all of you are graduating today not just with a great education," he continued, "but with the skills that will let you start your careers and skills that will make America stronger."

THE GROWING ROLE OF COMPUTERS IN FLIGHT

It certainly seems that computers are a part of every profession these days and aviation is no exception. Computers are an integral part of the job. They hold the blueprints, specifications, service orders, parts numbers, three-dimensional images, and everything else modern mechanics can use to make their jobs easier. Charles Horning, department chairman for the aviation maintenance science degree program at Embry-Riddle Aeronautical University told *Flying*, "[Students] may feel more like computer technicians than aircraft technicians."

For an aircraft mechanic, the key to using computers effectively is mobility. It is incredibly time consuming to keep leaving the craft in order to access a desktop or even a laptop computer. Many mechanics use tablet PCs, but those still

Modern diagnostic tools, software, and mobile technologies provide an entirely different toolkit for mechanics and technicians of the modern era.

require being held and having the mechanic looking down to see the screen. A growing number of mechanics have started using wearable computers. Michael Binko, vice president for the Xybernaut company, told *Aviation Pros* that wearable technology "allows employees to do more in less time, more accurately, or in a safer environment."

There are a few ways to wear computers. With one common technique, eyewear viewers attach to a person's eyeglasses or safety glasses and are connected to the main computer system.

Workers can access what they need and still keep their heads up and hands free. Tony Ho, director of business development at the company MicroOptical, says, "You have a productivity gain by having information right in front of the worker. It's a new paradigm in productivity, instead of going back and forth to your computer workstation or calling someone on the phone, you have the information directly in front of you. The idea is to access information anytime anywhere."

Airliners that fly for five, ten, or even twenty years often need parts switched out, including crucial ones like engine turbines. Routine inspections help the technicians determine if and when to replace equipment.

Companies such as FedEx frequently use these types of computers. According to Binko, "They bring aircraft in on a regular basis to be maintained and what would typically take several hours is cut down significantly. So if you multiply that out by how many aircraft they have and how many technicians, the results hit the bottom line pretty quickly and get noticed by the chief operating officer and chief financial officer."

Without leaving the aircraft, mechanics can ask about a part's availability, find out if it's already in inventory, and, if not, put in a request. As Binko adds, "If a technician is out in the field, they can describe in a 30-second sound bite what they're seeing. Or if you have photos you could attach them to your form . . . It's all about knowledge management, and delivery is the key return on that investment."

IN HIS BLOOD

When John Goglia was only fifteen years old, he solo piloted a small airplane. "I had been in love with airplanes since high school," he told the author. "When I was young, there weren't any fences around the airports, so I would ride my bike there and just

(continued on the next page)

27

(continued from the previous page)

watch the planes. It got into my blood—and then there was no leaving it."

Goglia has truly spent his entire life involved with aviation. As a full A&P aircraft mechanic for more than thirty years, he has written for multiple aviation trade publications and also coauthored two textbooks on air safety. In addition, Goglia is the first A&P mechanic to receive a presidential appointment to the National Transportation Safety Board (NTSB), where he served from 1995 to 2004. "I grabbed every opportunity that came my way," he explains.

It is clear that Goglia has enjoyed his career. "As an aircraft mechanic, you get to work anywhere in the world," he says. "If you want to travel, this is a great opportunity—and you get to work on the newest, most exciting planes. Sure, you work nights and weekends, and often in bad weather conditions, but it is all worth it."

"Aircraft mechanic is a great job," Goglia adds. "The pay is climbing, especially with the major airlines. It can reach $100,000 a year." Goglia admits the profession is a male-dominated one but says women do very well in it. He is part of an organization that provides scholarships to licensed female mechanics. When Goglia looks back on his years spent in air safety he says, "It was always full of surprises, and I can't complain."

IN THE COMMUNITY

Once you've explored what your school and the schools throughout the area have to offer, keep looking. Does your city have an airport, for example? Look online and research the airport's website for information on who to contact to ask some questions. Check if there is any kind of volunteer program in place. If there is, send in a professional cover letter, résumé, and anything else the site requires. If you are accepted, you probably will not be working with the mechanics but helping inside the airport itself. It may not be your first choice, but it is a first step in that direction.

If your city or area has a small, regional airport or airfield, you might want to stop in and ask some questions directly. For example, you could find out when they might be hiring, and if they accept volunteers or part timers. Someone who pops in occasionally and leaves a résumé and information may be the first person called if an opportunity arises. Small transportation hubs are great places to find mentors and get in on the ground floor of a career.

Do not wait to start exploring what your future might hold. Perhaps long-time aircraft mechanic Joe Loccisano said it best when he was interviewed on Gray Stone Advisors website, an aviation company. He became an A&P mechanic at the age of twenty-two, right after getting out of the US Air Force. "I always admired the complexities of aircraft and their systems," he says. "I was amazed watching it all work together on the platform. I wanted to learn as much as possible so I could become an 'expert' one day. I always thought that when you decide what you want to be in life," Loccisano added, "it should be something you love doing, not something you feel like you have to do or settle for."

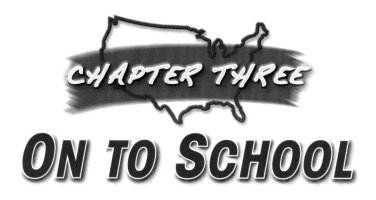

CHAPTER THREE

ON TO SCHOOL

There are several different pathways to becoming an aircraft mechanic—and just like when flying, some routes are faster and some routes are a little bit bumpier. The basic requirements to become a service technician are pretty clear. You have to be at least eighteen years old and able to read, write, speak, and understand English. You also should be a responsible person. As Spartan College of Aeronautics and Technology states on its website:

> **The work you'll do as an airline mechanic can literally mean life or death to someone. You need to be capable of having this in the front of your mind at all times, so you'll never be tempted to cut corners. Should something happen to a plane you have worked on owing to your carelessness, it's you the National Transportation Safety Board will be coming to see.**

If you meet these requirements, it is time to get certification. Generally, there are three main options to obtain it.

Pretty much every school that teaches aircraft mechanics and technicians will have real planes and equipment to work on, hopefully in up-to-date facilities.

OPTION ONE: APPRENTICESHIPS

The first option for working toward certification is to become an apprentice. You will have to be on the job for eighteen months for either an A or P certificate or thirty months to earn both. Your time must be spent under the direct supervision of someone who has an FAA mechanic's license. You will also have to provide proof of the work you have done (including pay stubs and a letter from your employer) before you will be allowed to take the required tests.

The apprentice route often appeals to young people because of the lower cost. Plus, it seems less complicated, generally. Keep in mind, however, that this route also means that you will not be authorized to approve planes, engines, appliances, or parts to be returned to service. Someone with a license will need to do that. This route tends to take a bit longer than others, since one usually has to be an apprentice for some time.

MILITARY TRAINING

A second choice is to get training through the military. Just being in the military is not enough, however. You have to make sure you are placed in one of the specific military jobs approved by the FAA. That list is available from the FAA Flight Standards District office. Since the list changes regularly, it is essential to get the most up-to-date one.

The US Air Force (USAF) offers more than fifty job specializations that qualify candidates for working on airplanes. The US Army has about twenty. Keep in mind that the military has its own specific requirements that you need to meet in order to enlist. For example, you will need to pass mandatory drug tests, be within a specific age range, and be in adequate mental and physical condition. When you leave the military, you should get an official letter from a superior stating what types of aircraft and engines you worked on, plus how many hours of work (not training) you put in.

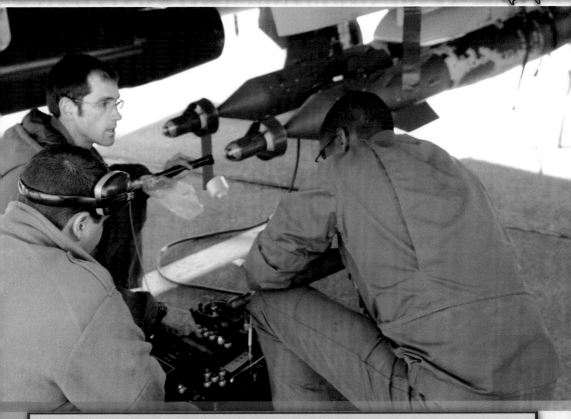

The various branches of the US military are well known for providing advanced training for aircraft mechanics and technicians, who are often exposed to cutting-edge technology before its rollout to civilian aviation.

SCHOOL'S IN

The third option to becoming an aircraft mechanic is to go to a school geared specifically toward this career. There are 170 aviation maintenance technician schools throughout the United States that are approved by the FAA. These schools offer courses in airframe (A), power plants (P), or both (A&P). An A or P certification takes eighteen months, while getting an A&P certification requires thirty months. These programs vary widely in price depending on the school. For example, Portland Community College in Oregon charges $8,500 for tuition and fees for the A&P certification, while Columbus State Community College in Ohio charges $14,000 (for in-state residents). The Aviation Institute of Maintenance in California currently charges $17,897 for both in- and out-of-state students.

THE TOP 10 AVIATION TECHNOLOGY SCHOOLS IN THE UNITED STATES

Where are the best aviation technology schools in the country? It largely depends on who you ask and which sites you visit online or which rankings you accept. Some of the schools that tend to appear the most often include:

- Purdue Polytechnic School of Aviation and Transportation and Technology (Indiana)

- University of North Dakota's John D. Odegard School of Aerospace Sciences (North Dakota)

- San Jose State University's College of Engineering and Department of Aviation and Technology (California)

- Embry-Riddle Aeronautical University (California and Arizona)

- Academy College (Minnesota)

- Spartan College of Aeronautics and Technology (Oklahoma)

- Aerosim Flight Academy (Florida)

- Pittsburgh Institute of Aeronautics (Pennsylvania, Maryland, Ohio, and South Carolina)

- University of Alaska (Alaska)

- Reedley College (California)

If you decide to pursue a bachelor's degree in aviation maintenance rather than just a certification, that process takes four years and can set you back from $20,000 to $80,000. A four-year degree takes longer and costs more, but it also means that, upon graduating, you are able to work not only as an aviation mechanic, but also as an aircraft salesperson, technical representative, or ground operations worker.

Whether one gets their training and education via an apprenticeship, military service, or a technical school, in the

Whatever educational route you choose to break into a new career, it's a safe bet that you will encounter several exams during your journey.

end they will have to take the exact same tests. There are three kinds: a written examination, an oral test, and a practical test. They cover a total of forty-three technical topics, including aircraft drawings, aircraft components, safety and ground operations, tools and measuring devices, and electricity. To pass, students must get at least 70 percent on each section. If you fail part of a test, you have to wait thirty days before getting the chance to take it again. All three tests have to be passed within a two-year period. There are a number of test prep courses out there for these exams, and they range in price from $150 to $500. In addition, there is a fee to take each exam, which ranges from $100 to $600.

TESTS AND MORE TESTS

The three tests (general, airframe, and power plant) cover all of the technical subjects and each one takes about eight hours to complete. Oral questions are asked about a variety of topics. The practical exam allows you to show what you have learned about basic airframe and power plants tasks and repairs. Students are often asked to do engine and electrical troubleshooting to show what they have learned. All relevant manuals will be available to students to access during the testing. The following are some sample questions from the test.

1. When inspecting a composite panel using the ring test/ tapping method, a dull thud may indicate
   a. less than full strength curing of the matrix.
   b. separation of the laminates.
   c. an area of too much matric between fiber layers.

2. The auxiliary (tail) rotor of a helicopter permits the pilot to compensate for and/or accomplish which of the following?
   a. Attitude and airspeed.
   b. Lateral and yaw position.
   c. Torque and directional control

3. The purpose of pressurizing aircraft cabins is to
   1. create the proper environment for prevention of hypoxia.

(continued on the next page)

(continued from the previous page)

    2. permit operation at high altitudes.
       Regarding the above statements,
       a. Only No. 1 is true.
       b. Only No. 2 is true.
       c. Both No. 1 and No. 2 are true.

4. When installing a DME antenna, it should be aligned with the
    a. null position.
    b. angle of incidence.
    c. centerline on the airplane.

5. When handling a high voltage capacitor in an electrical circuit, be sure it
    a. has a full charge before removing it from the circuit.
    b. has at least a residual charge before removing it from the circuit.
    c. is fully discharged before removing it from the circuit.

If you would like to see what the test prep books for these exams are like, check out the FAA's guide online.

IN THE CLASSROOM

What classes you take in aviation school depend on which type of certification you are pursuing (airframe, power plant, or both). Some of the most common classes taken, however, include the typical general education classes (English, history, science, and math), as well as courses in:

DEPARTMENT OF TRANSPORTATION
FEDERAL AVIATION ADMINISTRATION
ORVILLE WRIGHT BUILDING

The Federal Aviation Administration (FAA), headquartered in Washington, DC, as part of the US Department of Transportation, is one of the main bodies in charge of overseeing rules that aviation mechanics follow.

- Aviation basics
- Aircraft electricity
- Hydraulics and landing gear
- Writing
- Sheet metal
- Structures
- Aircraft drawings
- Ignition and starting systems
- Physics
- Chemistry
- Electronics
- Computer science
- Mechanical drawing

The process of becoming an aircraft mechanic can be done several ways. Once you have chosen between becoming an apprentice, joining the military, or going to school, another decision needs to be made. Do you want to pursue an airframe or power plant certification—or both?

CHAPTER FOUR

A&P: AIRFRAME AND POWER PLANT

Now that you have figured out your likely path to becoming an aircraft mechanic or service technician, it is time to decide if you want to pursue a single certification in either airframe or power plant or one that covers both. It depends on several factors. These include how much money you want to spend, how long you want to be a student or apprentice (eighteen versus thirty months), and what type of work appeals to you the most.

Both airframe and power plant mechanics are expected to learn many of the same skills, including basic electricity, aircraft drawings, weights and balances, corrosion control, maintenance forms and records, and fluid lines and fitting. However, after that the two types of certifications differ.

Airframe mechanics tend to focus on the physical fabric of the airplane. They are responsible for repairing, maintaining, and inspecting the wheels, wings, doors, windows, landing gear and brakes, floors, and outer "skin" of the plane. They are also responsible for the various mechanical systems, like lighting, heating and cooling, and hydraulic and pneumatic power systems. When it comes to the cockpit, they also help fix and maintain issues with communication and navigation, fuel delivery, ice and rain control, and much more.

The front landing gear assembly of a wide-body plane is shown here. Many mechanics get general training on a variety of aircraft systems, while others develop specialized areas of focus and are deployed for specialized jobs.

On the other hand, power plant mechanics focus on repairing, maintaining, and inspecting the engines (reciprocating and turbine) on the aircraft. These include systems that involve: helping the pilots track whether engines are operating properly; lubrication, ignition, and fuel distribution and metering; induction (the parts that direct air into the engine); engine cooling and exhaust; and propellers, turbines, and other locomotion systems. An A&P certificate means you have studied all of these topics. It's not surprising that the training period is thirty months!

Take a look at one example of the course schedule from the University of Alaska's website. You can see where a number of the classes overlap.

Course Title	Airframe	Power Plant
Aircraft Ground Operations and Safety	✓	✓
Basic Aerodynamics	✓	✓
Aircraft Publications, Regulations, and Records	✓	✓
Fundamentals of Aircraft Electronics/Lab	✓	✓
Drawing and Precision Measurement	✓	✓
Aircraft Materials and Processes I	✓	✓
Aircraft Fuel Systems/Lab	✓	✓
Aircraft Sheet Metal Structures/Lab	✓	
Aircraft Nondestructive Inspection Methods	✓	✓
Aircraft Electrical Hardware and Systems	✓	✓
Aircraft Fluid Power Systems/Lab	✓	
Aircraft Electronic Systems/Lab	✓	✓
Aircraft Auxiliary Systems/Lab	✓	
Aircraft Bonded Structures/Lab	✓	
Aircraft Materials and Processes II	✓	
Aircraft Avionics Systems	✓	
Airframe Assembly and Inspections Lab	✓	
Reciprocating Engine Theory		✓
Turbine Engine Theory		✓
Aircraft Reciprocating Engine Overhaul/Lab		✓
Aircraft Turbine Engine Repair and Overhaul/Lab		✓
Aircraft Propeller Systems		✓
Aircraft Electrical Machinery/Lab		✓
Reciprocating Engine Installation and Operation/Lab		✓
Turbine Engine Installation and Operation/Lab		✓

A FUTURE WITH AERIAL APPLICATORS

In the past, agricultural, or "ag," pilots were often known as crop dusters. Today, these pilots are known as aerial applicators. Then and now, their job is to fly at low altitudes in order to spray pesticides or fertilizers onto farmers' crops. The aircraft sometimes

(continued on the next page)

A crop dusting airplane dumps water as part of an airshow demonstration. A steady demand for mechanics to maintain and pilots to fly these planes makes it another career niche to choose from.

(continued from the previous page)

doubles as a water bomber in emergency wildfire situations. Some have even helped clean oil spills on the coast or destroyed harmful insects in forests. These high-tech planes often feature very expensive equipment such as million-dollar turbine engines and complex GPS systems. This allows the pilots to fly very precisely, with accuracy within three feet (nine meters). As Mike Linn wrote in *USA Today*, "Modern planes can cost upward of $1 million and spray at speeds near 150 miles per hour. They fly ten feet above fields during application, just low enough to make the most stoic of NBA stars duck for cover."

Because of this sophisticated equipment, a growing number of large agricultural firms, as well as individual ag pilots, are always searching for a skilled mechanic or service technician to keep everything in top working order.

GETTING HIRED

After finishing school and passing all the tests, it is time for the next challenge: finding a job. Most aircraft mechanics work in either a repair station or in an airport hangar. It is common, especially in the earlier years, to work both weekends and night shifts. The average annual income for aircraft mechanics depends on where they are located, how large the company is, how large the airport is, and what type of certification the mechanic has.

What's the best strategy to ace an interview for a position as an aircraft mechanic or service technician? Much of the advice is the same as it would be for any other type of job interview: be punctual, dress nicely, be polite, do some thoughtful research,

As with any job search, getting hired to fix or maintain aircraft depends not only on one's degrees, certifications, and skills, but also one's personality, politeness, and professionalism during interviews.

and practice ahead of the interview. Some common questions that interviewers throw out to candidates may include:

- How do you handle yourself in a stressful situation?
- Describe a time you had a conflict with another employee. How was it resolved?
- What is your greatest strength/biggest weakness?
- Why should we choose you to join our company?
- Do you prefer working in a team environment or independently?

BEYOND THE TRADITIONAL

When you picture an aircraft mechanic or service technician, chances are you picture someone standing underneath a big jet plane reaching deep into the darkness of the engine compartment. However, a number of these mechanics work on machines that do fly—but not in the traditional ways.

Some aircraft mechanics are needed to work on gliders or sailplanes. These may look like simple machines—and they are when compared with complex, computer-controlled jet planes—but they still need regular maintenance. Mechanics are frequently needed to repair crushed wings or fuselages, replace landing gear, or repair fuel tanks. They also provide annual inspections, all from certified repair stations. Other aircraft mechanics specialize in repairing and maintaining helicopters. This requires the ability to work on piston or reciprocating engines, as well as gas turbines. Helicopter mechanics perform pre-flight and post-flight inspections, carefully examining the engine and its components, as well as the rotor blades, exhaust carriers, and the overall body of the helicopter. Everything is required to meet FAA regulations.

Some aircraft mechanics take courses in unmanned aircraft systems as well. A major reason is one class of aircraft that are becoming increasingly popular: drones. Drones are defined as "aerial vehicles that can fly autonomously or be piloted by a remote individual." Experts predict that both consumers and the Department of Defense will be using drones in the air and civilian airspace in great numbers over the coming years. Some people will use them for fun, but drones will also be used for aerial photography and remote viewing and surveillance. Some schools, like the Aviation Institute of Maintenance, are offering classes for mechanics in just how to make sure these unmanned aircraft stay in good working order.

Believe it or not, some aircraft mechanics and service technicians are also called on to work on rollercoasters, dentists' chairs, and medical equipment! Some are even employed at Disney, Universal Studios, and NASCAR.

However, there are some questions that are specific to the position and you need to be ready to answer them. Examples include:

- What subject during your A&P training was your strongest?
- What do you excel at as an aircraft maintenance technician?
- What part of the aircraft do you find the most challenging to inspect and work on?
- How important is clear and detailed documentation to you?
- In what situation would you work on an airplane without proper engineer's authorization?

You've taken the classes and passed the test. With some hard work, you've finally found a job! Now it's time to remember that your A&P certification is truly a "license to learn." Working the job, day after day, is where the most important lessons will come. So enjoy, work hard, and learn! You've earned it.

CHAPTER FIVE

BEYOND A&P

Choosing a career can be hard. If you are going to invest your time, money, and hard work in something, you want to give certain choices a great deal of thought. Potential salary and benefits, the kind of training required, and the likely working conditions are important considerations. You already have some guidance on how to prioritize those. However, once someone has become an A&P mechanic, what are the next steps in one's career? The best jobs are those that allow you to improve, grow, and advance. Fortunately, this is a career ripe with opportunity.

After you have been an A&P mechanic for three years, you might want to consider adding "inspector's authorization" to your résumé. Holding an IA license allows you to inspect and approve major repairs on airplanes so that they can return to service. Stan Cates got his IA license in 1996. He obtained it because it seemed like the right step to take. "It was a sense of pride," he tells *Aviation Pros*. "It was also to help further my career in aviation." Aircraft mechanic Howard Sidlecki agrees,

Working as an A&P mechanic is a great career. If you want to go further, work on getting an inspector's authorization license.

saying, "For me, it boiled down to being the best mechanic I could be. It was the next logical step for me in my career."

To get an IA license and thus use your new skills professionally, you have to pass a test. It consists of fifty multiple-choice questions to be completed within three hours. Unlike the airframe and power plant exams, there are no oral or practical questions on this test. The minimum score to pass is seventy. There are prep courses and books available to help students prepare for the exam. Cates relied on a study guide to help him get ready, according to *Aviation Pros*. "It really helped me out. . . it would give different scenarios that would help develop research skills." Others prefer to learn directly from experts. Sidlecki states, "I was fortunate to work with an old-timer. The guy was a great source of knowledge, and he mentored me. I learned a lot from him."

WHAT'S IN A WORD?

What are some of the most commonly used terms in the world of aircraft mechanics? Here are some to know:

- ∅ A check: A regular check that is required after so many flight hours.
- ∅ AOG: Aircraft on ground; a plane prevented from flying because of a problem requiring repair.
- ∅ Airframe: The physical framework of an airplane such as the wings, wheels, cabin, doors, windows, brakes, lighting, etc.
- ∅ Avionics mechanic: A person who specializes in the electronic and control systems and components of an aircraft.
- ∅ B check: A regular check that is required every four to six months.
- ∅ Base maintenance: More complex repairs that

(continued on the next page)

(continued from the previous page)

will take some time.

- ø C check: An extensive check performed every twenty to twenty-four months.
- ø Cycle: One take off and one landing.
- ø Expendable: An aircraft part that can only be used once, such as oil.
- ø Line maintenance: Repairs, usually minor, that can be performed outside of a hangar.
- ø Maintenance logbook: A journal, required by the FAA, of any work that has been done on an aircraft. It should include the date, as well as the mechanic's name and certificate number.
- ø Power plant: The engine and fuel delivery systems of an airplane.
- ø Rotable: An aircraft part that can be repaired and returned to service, such as an engine.
- ø Work order: A schedule of work that creates the overall aircraft check.

GETTING A BACHELOR'S DEGREE

Some A&P mechanics may choose to get a bachelor's degree in aviation. A number of colleges offer these programs. At Embry-Riddle Aeronautical University's Daytona Beach campus, for example, they offer a bachelor of science degree in aviation maintenance. According to their website, students choose one of three areas of focus:

- **Flight:** This specialty is for students who want to combine a maintenance background with the qualifications of a commercial pilot.
- **Maintenance management:** This concentration is geared toward students who want to use their maintenance skills for moving into a management position in an aviation maintenance environment.
- **Safety science:** This course of study is for candidates who want to combine industrial and aviation-specific safety courses with a maintenance background.

In addition, A&P mechanics can earn certification in general radio telephone operation and as an aircraft electronics technician.

Thomas Education State University in Trenton, New Jersey, is another college that features a BS degree in aviation maintenance technology. Only A&P mechanics are allowed to take this course of study. Along with general education courses, students take classes on general aeronautics, avionics, and related electives such as weather, piloting, and thermodynamics.

At Everglades University in Boca Raton, Florida, students can take classes on many topics, including aviation security, airport management, federal aviation regulations, the history of aviation, introductory aeronautics, principles of supervision (management), aviation labor relations, and introductory space

Seeking a bachelor's degree in an aviation-related field will likely lead you to take a variety of classes in or related to the STEM fields.

studies. After years in the field, a number of A&P mechanics decide to share their advice, knowledge, and experience with others, so they become teachers at aviation schools. Others rise up to the position director of maintenance, or DOMs.

Another choice that some A&P mechanics are making today is to get cross-trained as flight technicians (FTs). According to *Flying*, a number of mechanics are learning to also function as FTs. These mechanics support and sometimes even replace flight attendants on specialized flights where maintenance might not

READING AND WRITING

It may not seem like being an aircraft service technician would involve spelling rules, good grammar, and comprehension skills, but it does. Aircraft technicians are required to understand everything they read in a variety of maintenance manuals, work orders, and endless lists of regulations and standards and be able to interpret and apply this content to their jobs. Not reading such documents thoroughly can lead to dangerous mistakes.

Anyone who maintains, performs preventative maintenance on, rebuilds, or alters an aircraft, engine, propeller, appliance, or component must provide clear, detailed, and accurate documentation. Spartan College of Aeronautics and Technology's website reminds students that aviation is a very highly regulated industry. The FAA, NTSB, and additional agencies keep a close eye on airports and aircraft maintenance shops. That means keeping proper paperwork. "There's a saying that all of the Federal Aviation Regulations are 'written in blood'—meaning that they became necessary after someone died because of a lack of regulation," Spartan explains. "While the point of a particular

(continued on the next page)

(continued from the previous page)

reporting procedure may not be readily obvious to you, someone further up the chain may find it very useful indeed. If you can consider the bureaucratic intrusions as part of the cost of getting to do what you love—make airplanes fly—then you have the right mindset for becoming an airline mechanic."

The FFA requires maintenance logs to have:

- The name of the mechanic
- A description of the work performed
- The total time in service on each part of the plane
- The current status of life-limited parts in the plane since the last time the plane's parts were overhauled
- The date of completion of the work done
- The signature, certificate number, and kind of certificate held by the person approving the work when finished

Mistakes can mean something is not repaired correctly and that can have dire results for everyone.

be available on the ground. Examples of these might include military flights, Air Force One, and private corporate jets. "It is a financial decision, based on skills and services the employee brings to the table," says Elaine Lapotsky, former president of the National Business Aviation Association's Flight Technicians and Flight Attendants Committee.

FTs are taught everything from how to serve airport food so it looks somewhat appetizing to how to fix a malfunctioning computer router while still in flight. In addition, they learn how to put out fires, secure the cabin in case of a crash landing, and get passengers off the plane safely in an emergency situation. FTs are shown how to deal with hazmat issues, hijacking attempts, and sudden illness or injury. They literally can "fix and fly."

CHAPTER SIX

INTO THE FUTURE

*L*ike many other fields today, the aircraft mechanic and service technician profession is working to increase the overall diversity of their crews. One area being focused on is hiring more women. For women interested in becoming A&P mechanics, there is good news and bad news. The bad news is that there are not very many of them. Experts estimate less than 5 percent of the country's aircraft mechanics are women. The good news is that this is changing—just ask these A&P licensed mechanics.

WELCOMING WOMEN

"A lot of people are caught off guard by the girl in overalls with lip gloss and a pink Snap-on screwdriver in her pocket heading out on the ramp to fuel their plane," Toni Breese told the *Peninsula Clarion*. "Tourists have asked to take my picture when I'm down on the dock working on a plane during the summer."

Although Breese had originally pursued a career as a medical aesthetician, she ended up changing course. "Off and on over the years, from my late teens until becoming a mechanic, I have thought about and researched the A&P career," she states. "As a woman in the industry, I tend to see things different than the guys, which can be a great advantage. As a woman, I will see a completely different way to do something, repair or approach a situation," she explains. "It's worked for me so far and I'm excited to see where this road leads."

Stacy Rudser was introduced to the idea of becoming an aircraft mechanic by an Air Force major. She received a scholarship from UPS Airlines through the Association for Women in Aviation Maintenance. "That scholarship changed my career," she told *Air and Space*. Rudser loves her job. "It's always different," she explains. "Even if an airplane has the same problem that you ran into the other day, it might have a different cause. Also seeing the [new] engines they're coming out with. . . It's brilliant. It's like being in a sci-fi novel sometimes."

While still in high school, Jenn McBeth got her pilot's license. Flying was wonderful, but she was also intrigued by the mechanics behind it. Today, she works for a flight company in Tukwila, Washington. She loves her job, but worked hard to gain acceptance as a woman in a very male profession. "I've been in situations where I haven't had an ally," she shares with Channel K5 in Washington. "Being a woman in this field, for whatever reason, is either offensive or uncomfortable to people." Fortunately, McBeth's employer did not feel that way. In fact, Ira Woyar wishes he had more mechanics like her. "She's got a fabulous attitude, a hard worker, good attention to detail, shows up at her job every day, does it well. I couldn't ask for anything better," he adds. "She's sharp."

McBeth admitted that she had to learn a lot for this job. "What I've done in aviation, it's all learned, I'm not a natural

While it may have been uncommon a few decades ago to encounter women as mechanics or managers, the modern airline industry has slowly begun to level the playing field for them.

mechanic wiz," she said. "I think especially for women, you can find the trap of thinking 'I'm not naturally mechanical, so that whole field of the entire world is closed off to me.'" Even though McBeth's supervisor believes she could be director of operations for an air carrier in a short period, McBeth is happy with what she is doing right now. "Work on planes, fly them, and just keep doing that more and better!" As more companies expand the diversity of their hiring practices, it will get easier for women to find jobs in the aircraft safety field.

A LONG CAREER

As an airline mechanic for American Airlines, Azriel Blackman has some definite limitations. He has to stay off of ladders, cannot drive out onto Kennedy International Airport's airfield, and isn't even allowed to use any tools. Nonetheless, he is a very important employee. As crew chief, he is responsible for reviewing all of the copious paperwork showing what work has been done—and what still needs to be done—on various jetliners. He is closely monitored by a crew cochief. Robert Needham, maintenance manager and Blackman's boss, told the *New York Times*, "He loves coming to work. His work ethic is something I'd love every one of my 368 mechanics here to have."

What truly makes Blackman unusual is not just that he is a dedicated worker. It is the fact that he turned ninety-two in 2017. He started his career as an A&P mechanic in 1942, at the age of sixteen. He holds the Guinness World Record for the longest career as an airline mechanic. "Every day the job is different," Blackman stated. "You're not doing the same thing repetitively, and that's good. If, in my journey around the hangar, I see something I can help on, I do that." Everything Blackman does is carefully supervised.

(continued on the next page)

(continued from the previous page)

"With the airline sensitive to maintenance and FAA guidelines and everything else," explained Needham, "we always have to be careful what he's doing." Robert Crandall, former president of American Airlines, believes that the skills and knowledge Blackman has to offer are "incalculable." He added, "He represents a valuable institutional memory that says, 'This is how we do it at American.' . . . This is how you pass it on to the next generation. He's the guy who sits with the new kids at lunch and passes it on."

In 2017, American Airlines mechanic Azriel Blackman not only turned ninety-two years old but also marked a record seventy-five years of employment with the air carrier.

A GREAT FEELING

Becoming an A&P mechanic or service technician can be challenging if you are dealing with certain disabilities. Being physically fit and able to climb, bend, stretch, and lift are all important qualifications for the job. However, Zackary Kukorlo got his license and did not let his deafness become an obstacle. He didn't stop there, however. Through a program at Indiana's Purdue University, Kukorlo also took steps to become a pilot.

Kukorlo has dreamt of being a pilot since he was five years old, he relayed to *Inside Indiana Business* magazine. He knew it would not be easy because of his hearing loss. "You have to find another way to communicate with signals or to set up two-way communication through texting or something like that," he explained. "But there are also signals from the tower; when you see the light, you know it's clear to land and clear to take off."

During training, Kukorlo's instructor sat next to him in order to use hand signals or write notes. Although the young mechanic wants to eventually fly commercial jets, he knows that will be a battle. "You freak people out if their pilot is deaf," he said, "so I've decided to stick with cargo." Moving all the way up to becoming an airline transport pilot is Kukorlo's dream. "It'd be a long, gradual stepping up," he admitted. "This has been my dream my whole life to do this. I believe my disability won't prevent me, but legally, it might [be difficult]. I'll try my hardest to break through this. It would be a great feeling."

AVIATION TECHNICIAN OF THE YEAR

How does a person earn the title of National Aviation Technician of the Year? It isn't easy because there is a great deal of competition. In 2017, the winner was Brian John Carpenter from Corning, Montana. Not only has Carpenter spent his lifetime involved with aircraft mechanics, but he has developed a specialty and helped countless others in the process.

When Carpenter was quite young, he flew remote-controlled aircraft. In junior high, he built a self-launching glider and tried jumping off small hills in an attempt to fly. As an adult, Carpenter earned his A&P and pilot certification, and in 1991, he opened his own aviation company. Although the company inspected and maintained different types of aircraft, Carpenter specialized in his favorite: light sport aircraft. Not only did he help maintain these small crafts, he also taught others how to fly them and built his own models. He has trained others throughout the United States and in Australia and has written articles and books on the topic. He teaches workshops, leads seminars, and produces educational videos. Carpenter has even designed an electric motor glider and more than one hundred 3D printed parts for use on aircraft. No wonder he is tech of the year!

A STRONG OUTLOOK

How promising the future of aircraft mechanics is seems to depend largely on who you ask. The Bureau of Labor Statistics does not see much growth. It states that there will be little change between now and 2024. As older, worn aircraft are phased out and replaced with new, high-tech planes, less overall maintenance will be needed. However, some experts in the field have different opinions.

The skills that airplane mechanics develop are transferable anywhere in the world. Here, a team of workers and engineers at Lufthansa Technik breaks down an airplane in Sofia, Bulgaria.

In a *Forbes* magazine article, experts from Oliver Wyman, a global management consulting firm, stated that there is a definite gap between the number of available mechanics and the demand for them. They think that problem will only continue to grow for the next decade. In part, this is because of the fact that a high number of today's maintenance technicians are "baby boomers." According to the Bureau of Labor Statistics, the median age of mechanics in 2017 is fifty-one years old, so retirement is only a few years away. As these veterans retire, some worry there will not be enough new mechanics to take their places.

Wyman predicts that globally, the airline industry will be adding more than ten thousand planes to its fleet by 2027. They also state that by that time, more than half of the world's fleet will be made up of aircraft designed and built after the year 2000. "Mechanics moving forward will need the skill sets to work not only on the newest planes, but also ones that that have been flying for more than 20 years—and these are not necessarily the same," Wyman stated. "This requirement further complicates the shortage; when supply and demand are right, employers have to hope that the right mechanics with the right skill sets are in the right place at the right time when needed."

Do you think you might have what it takes? If so, there is no time like the present to start on the path of becoming an aircraft mechanic or technician and be part of one of the most dynamic and rewarding technical fields out there.

Bureau of Labor Statistics Tips

What They Do	Work Environment	How to Become One	Job Outlook
• Diagnose mechanical or electrical problems • Repair wings, brakes, electrical systems, and other aircraft components • Replace defective parts, using hand tools or power tools • Examine replacement aircraft parts for defects • Read maintenance manuals to identify repair procedures • Test aircraft parts with gauges and other diagnostic equipment • Inspect completed work to ensure that it meets performance standards • Keep records of maintenance and repair work	• Hangars • Repair Stations • Airfields	• Specific military service • Apprenticeship • 18 or 30 month trade school program • Passing grade on three exams (written, oral, and practical)	• Little to no change between now and 2024

GLOSSARY

apprentice A person who gains skills in a trade by studying under the close supervision of senior professionals.

auditing Sitting in on a class without officially enrolling in it.

avionics The study of electronics and their use in aircraft.

baby boomer Somebody born in the postwar era of the late 1940s through the 1950s and early 1960s.

corrosion A natural process of gradual destruction of certain materials, like metals.

critical infrastructure Systems and assets vital to a country, such that their destruction would have a debilitating impact on security, the economy, public health, or safety.

cross-train To train for multiple jobs or sports.

disability A mental or physical condition that limits someone's physical movement or senses in some way.

diversity In employment and other sectors of society, the effort to be inclusive and have many varieties of people working, studying, or otherwise interacting with each other.

hazmat A common abbreviation of "hazardous material."

hydraulic Refers to mechanisms that are powered by fluids being forced through small holes or tubes.

pneumatic Describes mechanical systems that depend on compressed air for their motion.

stoic Patient and unemotional.

supervise To watch over and monitor to ensure something is being done properly.

survey To look at or examine something carefully.

turbines An engine that works by water, steam, or air pushing a series of spinning blades.

vocational Relating to job or career skills.

Aircraft Mechanics Fraternal Association (AMFA)
7853 E. Arapahoe Court, Suite 1100
Centennial, OH 80112
(303) 752-2632
Website: www.amfanational.org
Facebook: @AMFANational
The AMFA is a craft union representing employees working
in the repair and maintenance of aircraft.

Association for Women in Aviation Maintenance (AWAM)
2300 Kenlee Drive
Cincinnati, OH 45230
(386) 416-0248
Website: https://www.awam.org
AWAM is an association dedicated to helping women in
aviation maintenance find ways to network and support
each other in their field.

Federal Aviation Administration (FAA)
800 Independence Ave SW
Washington, DC 20591
(866) 835-5322
Website: http://www.faa.gov
Facebook: @FAA
The FAA is the main government agency overseeing commercial
airline safety and operations for the United States.

National Business Aviation Association (NBAA)
1200 G Street NW, Suite 100
Washington, DC 20005

(202) 783-9000
Website: http://www.nbaa.org
Twitter: @NBAA
Facebook: @NBAAfans
Founded in 1947 and based in Washington, DC, the NBAA
    is the leading organization for companies that rely on
    general aviation aircraft to help make their businesses
    more efficient, productive, and successful.

Organization of Black Aerospace Professionals
One Westbrook Corporate Center Suite 300
Westchester, IL 60154
(800) 538-6227
Website: https://obap.memberclicks.net
Facebook @OBAPMTSU
Founded in 1976, the Organization of Black Aerospace
    Professionals is a nonprofit organization dedicated to
    the encouragement and advancement of minorities in all
    aviation and aerospace careers.

Professional Aviation Maintenance Association (PAMA)
1601 Marlene Drive
Euless, TX 76040
(866) 699-7262
Website: http://pama.org
Facebook: @PAMANational
PAMA is dedicated to promoting professionalism and
    recognition of the aviation maintenance technician
    through communication, education, and representation
    and supports continuous improvement in aviation safety.

FOR FURTHER READING

Cinnamon, Ian, Romi Kadri, and Fitz Tepper. *DIY Drones for the Evil Genius: Design, Build, and Customize Your Own Drones.* New York, NY: McGraw Hill, 2016.

Dougherty, Martin. *Aircraft* (Modern Weapons Compared and Contrasted). New York, NY: Rosen Publishing, 2012.

Gibson, Karen Bush. *Women Aviators: 26 Stories of Pioneer Flights, Daring Missions, and Record-Setting Journeys.* Chicago, IL: Chicago Review Press, 2013.

Grant, Reg. *Flight: 100 Years of Aviation.* New York, NY: DK Publishing, 2010.

Greenhaven Press. *Drones* (Current Controversies). Farmington Hills, MI: Greenhaven Press, 2016.

Kallen, Stuart. *Careers in Aviation and Aerospace.* San Diego, CA: Reference Point Press, 2017

Murray, Laura. *Southwest Airlines* (Built for Success). Scituate, MA: Creative Education, 2015.

Sodomka, Martin. *How to Build a Plane: A Soaring Adventure of Mechanics, Teamwork, and Friendship.* Lake Forest, CA: Walter Foster Jr. Books, 2015.

Terwilliger, Brent, David Ison, and John Robbins. *Small Unmanned Aircraft Systems Guides: Exploring Designs, Operations, Regulations, and Economics.* Newcastle, WA: Aviation Supplies and Academics, 2017.

Weinick, Suzanne. *Careers in Aviation* (Essential Careers). New York, NY: Rosen Publishing, 2012.

BIBLIOGRAPHY

Aerospace Industries Association. "Aviation: A Critical Component of National Infrastructure." April 2017. https://www.aia-aerospace.org/report/aviation-a-critical -component-of-national-infrastructure.

Aviation Maintenance. "Drone Industry Outlook." September 26, 2017. http://www.aviationmaintenance.edu/blog/tag /continuing-education.

Aviation Maintenance. "Women in Aviation." March 31, 2014. http://www.aviationmaintenance.edu/blog/women -in-aviation/women-in-aviation.

Bright Work Polish. "Aircraft Maintenance Terms You Should Know." April 19, 2017. https://www.brightworkpolish .com/aircraft-maintenance-terms-you-should-know.

CareerMetis.com. "10 Things You Didn't Know about Becoming an Aircraft Mechanic." June 13, 2016. https:// www.careermetis.com/things-didnt-know-about -becoming-aircraft-mechanic.

"Corning Man Named Aviation Technician of the Year." *Daily News*, February 25, 2017. http://www.redbluffdailynews .com/article/ND/20170225/NEWS/170229912.

CostHelper Education. "Aircraft Mechanic Training Cost." Retrieved October 9, 2017. http://education.costhelper .com/aircraft-mechanic-school.html.

Erickson, Anne. "Kenmore Air Mechanic Loves Being a Woman in a Male-Dominated Trade." K5, April 25, 2017. http://www.king5.com/entertainment/television /programs/evening/kenmore-air-mechanic-loves-being-a -woman-in-a-male-dominated-trade/434106421.

Escobar, Joe. "Getting Your Inspection Authorization."
   Aviation Pros, March 1, 2004. http://www.aviationpros
   .com/article/10386639/getting-your-inspection
   -authorization.

Federal Aviation Administration. "Air Traffic by the Numbers."
   July 31, 2017. https://www.faa.gov/air_traffic/by_the
   _numbers.

Federal Aviation Administration. "General Aviation Airports:
   A National Asset." May 2012. https://www.faa.gov
   /airports/planning_capacity/ga_study
   /media/2012AssetReport.pdf.

Green, Jeff, and John Irwin. "Auto-Shop Class is a Win-
   Win for High School Grads, Dealerships that Need
   Mechanics." *Automotive News*, August 25, 2014. http://
   www.autonews.com/article/20140825
   /RETAIL05/140829934/auto-shop-class-is-a-win-win
   -for-high-school-grads-dealerships-that.

Hess, Alexander E. M., and Samuel Weigley. "The Nine Most
   Common Airplane Accidents." 24/7 Wall Street, April 24,
   2013. http://247wallst.com/special-report/2013/04/24
   /the-nine-most-common-airplane-accidents/3.

Interview with John Goglia, Aircraft Mechanic, October 3, 2017.

Interview with Luke Foreman, Aircraft Mechanic, via Email,
   October 4, 2017.

Jackinsky, McKibben. "Homer 'Girly Girl' Takes Path Few
   Women Follow as Licensed Airplane Mechanic." *Peninsula
   Clarion*, June 18, 2012. http://peninsulaclarion
   .com/news/2012-06-18/homer-%E2%80%98girly
   -girl%E2%80%99-takes-path-few-women-follow-as
   -licensed-airplane-mechanic.

Laboda, Amy. "You Bet Mechanics Can Fly!" *Flying*, January 13, 2017. http://www.flyingmag.com/you-bet-mechanics -can-fly.

Lara, Jim. "Aircraft Maintenance Leadership: An Interview with DOM Joe Loccisano." Gray Stone Advisors. Retrieved October 2, 2017. http://www.graystoneadvisors .com/aircraft-maintenance-leadership-dom-joe-loccisano.

Levensen, Michael. "3,200 Students on Vocational Education Wait Lists." *Boston Globe*, November 26, 2017. https:// www.bostonglobe.com/metro/2016/11/25 /students-vocational-education-wait-lists /JsfYrz5pvWTpqtZSINvQoL/story.html.

Linn, Mike. "Crop-Dusters Flying Off into the Sunset." *USA Today*, June 29, 2006. http://usatoday30.usatoday.com /news/nation/2006-06-29-crop-dusters_x.htm.

Maksel, Rebecca. "Airframe and Powerplant Mechanic." *Air and Space*, August 2017. https://www.airspacemag.com /as-next/01_aug2017-august-as-next-180963927.

Martinez, Sara. "Inside Iberia: A Day in the Life of Aircraft Mechanic Carlos Alonso." *Iberia Plus*, July 3, 2017. http://www.iberiaplusmagazine.iberia.com /articles/2017/7/inside-iberia-carlos-alonso.

Negroni, Christine. "For 75 Years, a Mechanic Has Helped Keep Planes Aloft." *New York Times*, July 17, 2017. https://www.nytimes.com/2017/07/17/nyregion/for -airline-mechanic-91-the-sky-is-one-of-many-limits.html.

Prentice, Brian, and Derek Constanza. "Aging Baby Boomers Cause Aircraft Mechanics Shortage as Global Fleet

Expands, Modernizes." *Forbes*, April 24, 2017. https://
www.forbes.com/sites/oliverwyman/2017/04/24/looming
-aircraft-mechanic-shortage-may-threaten-the-growth-of
-the-global-fleet-and-raise-costs/#6d943bff4984.

"Should You be an Aircraft Mechanic?" Spartan College
of Aeronautics and Technology blog, March 18, 2017.
https://www.spartan.edu/blog/should-you-be-an-aircraft
-mechanic.

University of Alaska Anchorage. "Undergraduate Certificate
in Aviation Maintenance Technology, Airframe." Retrieved
October 9, 2017. https://catalog.uaa.alaska.edu
/undergraduateprograms/ctc/aviationtechnology/certificate
-aviationmaintenancetechnologyamtairframe/#text.

University of Alaska Anchorage. "Undergraduate Certificate
in Aviation Maintenance Technology, Power Plant."
Retrieved October 9, 2017. https://catalog.uaa.alaska
.edu/undergraduateprograms/ctc/aviationtechnology
/certificate-aviationmaintenancetechnologypowerplant.

US Department of Transportation. "FAA: What We Do."
Retrieved October 4, 2017. https://www.faa.gov/about
/mission/activities.

Veleta, Kylie. "Deaf A&P Mechanic Earns His Wings." *Inside
Indiana Business*, August 9, 2017. http://www
.insideindianabusiness.com/story/36097184/deaf-ap
-mechanic-earns-his-wings.

Whitehouse.gov. "Remarks by the President at Worcester
Technical High School Commencement Ceremony." June
11, 2014. https://obamawhitehouse.archives.gov
/the-press-office/2014/06/11/remarks-president

-worcester-technical-high-school-commencement
-ceremony.

Wynbrandt, James. "Aviation Maintenance Technician Career
Profile." *Flying*, April 10, 2015. http://www.flyingmag
.com/careers/unique-aviation-career-aviation
-maintenance-technician.

Zuehike, Barb. "Wearable Computers: New Technology
Boosts Productivity in Aircraft Maintenance." *Aviation
Pros*, April 1, 2004. http://www.aviationpros.com
/article/10386608/wearable-computers-new-technology
-boosts-productivity-in-aircraft-maintenance.

INDEX

ABOUT THE AUTHOR

Tamra Orr is the author of numerous nonfiction books for readers of all ages, including multiple career books for Rosen Publishing. She graduated from Ball State University in Muncie, Indiana, and currently lives in the Pacific Northwest with her family. She has to fly often for her work, and each time she does, she takes a minute to mentally thank the aircraft mechanics and service technicians for doing such a great job.

PHOTO CREDITS

Cover, pp. 3, 12 Mehmet Cetin/Shutterstock.com; p. 6–7, 25 Monty Rakusen/Cultura/Getty Images; p. 10 VanderWolf Images /Shutterstock.com; p. 14 Ryan Fletcher/Shutterstock.com; p. 17 Pressmaster/Shutterstock.com; pp. 19, 54 Hero Images /Getty Images; p. 23 Compassionate Eye Foundation/Steven Errico /DigitalVision/Getty Images; pp. 26, 31 aapsky/Shutterstock.com; p. 33 Stephan Agostini/AFP/Getty Images; p. 36 Tom Wang /Shutterstock.com; p. 39 B Christopher/Alamy Stock Photo; p. 41 Andrey Khachatryan/Shutterstock.com; p. 43 Mislik /Shutterstock.com; p. 45 MR. Nattanon Kanchak /Shutterstock.com; p. 50 Bloomberg/Getty Images; p. 60 Konstantin Pelikh/Alamy Stock Photo; p. 62 Chang W. Lee/The New York Times/Redux; p. 65 Stoyan Yotov/Shutterstock.com; interior pages background (engine) TungCheung/Shutterstock.com.

Design: Nelson Sá; Layout: Nicole Russo-Duca; Editor: Phil Wolny; Photo Researcher: Ellina Litmanovich